Collaborator

"Get *education*. It will make you independent and powerful!"

Savitribai Phule (1831-1897) **collaborated** with several school systems and established the first girl's school in India in 1848.

Inspiring

"Dispel **ego** and **greed**. Remain *united.* Be *strong* and *brave."*

- *Jijabai Shahaji Bhosale (1598-1674)*, the Rajmata of Maratha Empire **inspired** her son, Chatrapati to become India's warrior King by teaching him bravery, determination, and integrity.

Grateful

"I am *grateful* to the problems in my life, because each
problem teaches me a new lesson!"

• *Anandi Gopalrao Joshi (1865-1887)* continued to become better by learning from the problems in her life and, in 1886, became one of the first woman physicians in India.

Believer in Self-Empowerment

"No matter what – one must *empower* themselves with education, act positively, and take charge of their lives!"

- *Muthulakshmi Reddi (1886-1968)* **empowered** herself by being the first Indian female student to graduate successfully from a men's medical college in 1907; became the first women house surgeon; established one of the biggest cancer institutes in India; and promoted women's equality.

Fierce

"When there is oppression, do not succumb. The only self-respecting thing is to rise and say, this shall cease today because my right is justice."

- *Sarojini Devi (1879-1949)* fought **fiercely** for civil rights and women's rights by writing poems!

Persistent

"Despite strong opposition, I *persisted* to shine!"

• *Anna Chandy (1905-1996)* **persistently** worked hard and became India's first female Judge in 1937.

Environmentalist

"We must *care for the trees* like we care for our children."

- The Green Grandma *Saalumarada Thimmakka (1910-2021)*, walked 2.5 miles every day to plant and care for 8385 trees.

Tenacious

"Every person has problems in their lives. Winners, *tenaciously* find out solutions to their problems, while others give up."

• *Kamala Sohonie (1911-1998)* was one of the first Indian female scientists to get a Ph.D. in 1939.

Energetic

"Always being *happy* and *cheerful* helped me tide over many problems in my life."

- **_Energetic_** _Sarla Thukral (1914-2008)_ was India's first woman pilot to fly an aircraft solo in 1936.

Leader

"Any little girl or a boy can become a *Super girl* or a *Super boy* with education, bravery, hard work, and by making the right choices in life."

- **Captain Lakshmi Sahgal** (1914-2012) was a gynecologist and the first lady officer in the Indian National Army. She **led** the all-women regiment, called the Rani of Jhansi Regiment, and fought for India's freedom.

Quiz

Q1. Why is Anandi Gopal Joshi grateful to the problems in her life? (pg.6)

A.

Q2. What are the winning qualities of pilot Sarla Thukral? (pg. 18)

A.

Q3. Of the following, what did Jijabai teach her son? (pg.4)
(a) Remain united
(b) Be brave and strong
(c) Don't be greedy
(d) All of the above

Quiz

Q4. What is integrity? (pgs.5; 36)

A.

Q5. According to Savitribai Phule, why do we need education?
   (pg. 2)

A.

Q6. According to the Green Grandma Saalumudra Thimmaka,
   what must we do for the trees? (pgs. 14; 15)

(a). care for the trees

(b). pluck the leaves

(c). plant the trees

(d). water the trees.

Quiz

Q7. Among the following, pick one or more ways *you want to* self-empower yourself: (pgs. 8; 9; 36)

(1) By getting educated
(2) Exercising
(3) Eating healthy
(4) Acting positively
(5) Being responsible for your life
(6) Making the right choices
(7) Getting a job
(8) Setting small goals and achieving them
(9) Smiling
(10) Praying.

Quiz

Q8. How will empowering yourself help you? (pgs. 8; 9; 36)

A.

Q.9. What did the judge Anna Chandy do when people opposed
   her? (pgs. 12; 13)

A.

Q10. What does a collaborator do? Why is it good to
collaborate? (pgs. 35; 3)

A.

Quiz

Q11. When winners face problems in their lives, what do they
do? (pgs. 16; 37)

A.

Q12. Why should one must dispel greed? (pgs. 4; 35)

A.

Q13. How can you become a Supergirl or a Superboy? (pg. 20)

A.

Quiz

Q. 14. What did you like and/or dislike about the book? Why?

A.

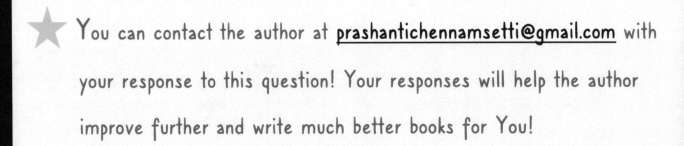 You can contact the author at **prashantichennamsetti@gmail.com** with your response to this question! Your responses will help the author improve further and write much better books for You!

COLORING PAGES

What will YOU do to change the world?

Glossary

Act Positively: Focusing on the good in a situation

Cease: To stop

Civil Rights: People's rights to equality and freedom

Collaborator: A person who works with others on a project

Conserve: To protect

Determination: Not giving up

Dispel: To get rid of; eliminate

Ego: A person who never accepts their mistakes

Fierce: To be strong; powerful

Grateful: To be thankful

Greed: Selfishly wanting more and more of something

Gynecologist: Doctors who specialize in women's health

Glossary

Idle: Avoiding work; being lazy

Inspiring: Encouraging

Integrity: Honesty

Justice: Fairness

Mighty: Strong; powerful; energetic; prestigious

Oppression: Bad treatment

Persistent: To be determined

Ph.D.: A doctoral degree is any subject

Rajmata: A queen who is a mother

Regiment: An Army unit, divided into several sections and led by an Army officer

Self-Empowerment: Taking steps to make your life better

Solo: An activity that's done by one person

Glossary

Succumb: To give in

Tenacious: Being determined;
strong-willed

Warrior: A brave soldier

About the Author

Prashanti Chennamsetti is a writer, teacher, and a social scientist. She was born and raised in India, where she got her master's degree in Applied Psychology. After that, she moved to the US and earned her doctoral degree in Educational Administration and Human Resource Development from Texas A&M University.

"The Mighty Ten: Ten Amazing Female Role Models from India" was inspired by this simple question from her kids, "Mama, don't we have any women superheroes from India?" That was when she decided to write this book—a book recognizing some of the incredible but lesser-known women in India's history.

Dr. Chennamsetti is a Gallup International Positive Psychology Fellow with several peer-reviewed journal publications to her credit. However, 'The Mighty Ten' is her first Children's book, which she wrote in the early morning hours, while enjoying the sounds of chirping birds, watching the beautiful dew drops on the leaves and drinking her favorite hot cacao. Through this book, she strives to bring a positive and compassionate mindset among children, contributing her part in making them global citizens, who are culturally aware.

During the book writing process, there came a time when the author got stuck, didn't know how to design the book. It was then that her kids came to her rescue and helped her design 'The Mighty Ten!' That's when she realized that children could do miracles!

She is grateful to the illustrator Mr. Garry Vaux for his diligence and artistic skills.

Made in the USA
Coppell, TX
12 May 2022